Ali Cat's
Magic Circle
Book of Tricks

Look-in Books

Also available in this series

RUNAROUND QUIZ BOOK
compiled by Robin May

THE FLOCKTON FLYER
Peter Whitbread

MAGPIE MAKE AND DO
Eileen Deacon

ROLF HARRIS ANIMAL QUIZ BOOK
Animals of the British Isles
compiled by Roy Harris

OUR LANDSCAPE
Discovering how it was made
Walter Shepherd

HOW — FUNTASTIC
Sue Dyer

STEWPOT'S FUN BOOK
Denis Gifford

BREAKTIME
Hazel Evans

BRIAN MOORE'S FOOTBALL QUIZ BOOK
Brian Moore

Ali Cat's Magic Circle Book of Tricks

Forty top tricks for beginners

*In association with the ITV series 'Magic Circle'
from HTV*

Illustrations by
Christine Howes

Cartoons by
Ann Axworthy

Jointly published by
INDEPENDENT TELEVISION BOOKS LTD
247 Tottenham Court Road, London W1P 0AU

and

ARROW BOOKS LTD
3 Fitzroy Square, London W1

An Imprint of the Hutchinson Publishing Group

London Melbourne Sydney Auckland
Wellington Johannesburg and agencies
throughout the world

First published 1977
© AZ Productions Ltd. 1977

ISBN: 0 09 915530 3

Made and printed in Great Britain
by The Anchor Press Ltd
Tiptree, Essex

Contents

A Message from Ali Cat

This book of magic is specially written and illustrated for beginners between the ages of seven and seventeen. You will have seen some of these tricks performed by magicians at magic shows and parties. Now you are going to be shown how they are performed so that you too can be a magician. Remember though that this book is a book of secrets. All I ask is that every girl and boy magician keep the secrets to themselves.

For a start, I am going to show you simple but effective tricks that anyone can perform, no matter how young. No special apparatus is needed and no difficult sleight of hand is involved.

Each trick occupies two pages. On the left-hand page is outlined the impact which the trick will have on your audience. On the right-hand side are the explanations, many of them illustrated, of how each trick is done.

As you proceed through the book some of the tricks reach professional standards, but they are still easy to perform, for simplicity is the secret of all good magic.

Ali Cat's Magic Circle Book of Tricks is the first of its kind. Although it is intended for younger beginners in the ancient art, many adults will find tricks worthy of their attention.

The secrets contained in these pages are not new. Some date back more than 2,000 years to the days of the Pharaohs. None the less, they *are* magical secrets. Many of them are used in the *Magic Circle* ITV series, produced under the auspices of the Magic Circle itself which is acknowledged to be the most exclusive magical society in the world. Members include such famed magicians as David Nixon, Johnny Hart, Robert Harbin, Tommy Cooper, David Berglas and many more.

The secrets revealed here are in daily use by many of the world's top magicians. Guard them well.

Meanwhile, for the novice, here are my GOLDEN DONT'S...

Don't attempt to perform any trick in public until you have practised it many times in private.

Don't attempt the more difficult tricks until you have mastered the easier ones.

Don't do the same trick twice. You may baffle your friends the first time; the chances are they won't be fooled as easily if they see it again immediately.

Don't do more than half a dozen tricks per show.

Don't try to entertain for more than five minutes. In my ITV series, *Magic Circle,* some of the world's top magicians were on the screen only for three minutes. Keep your performances short.

And, finally, the most important DON'T of all: *Don't* show your friends how the tricks are done.

Remember 'A secret is no longer a secret if it's known to everyone.'

Yours in Magic,
Ali Cat.

The Floating Cigar

What you do

You need to borrow a cigar for this clever little trick. It will work with a cigarette, but the chances are greater that your audience will then spot how it is done. Cigars are best — the bigger the better.

Take the unlit cigar and place it across the fingers of the right hand, palm upwards.

Pass your left hand mysteriously over the cigar, pronounce your favourite magic words and then swiftly turn over your right hand. The cigar remains sticking to your fingers. You can move your hand about freely, and the cigar still remains lying across your hand.

Take the clinging cigar away from your right hand and just return it to its owner with a smile and these words: 'You have a floating cigar there. A very rare item. Take great care of it.'

Say nothing more. Leave him puzzled.

How you do it

To stop the borrowed cigar from falling, you use a small pin. Stick the pin in the centre of the cigar as soon as you have borrowed it.

You will have plenty of time to do this when you turn your back on the audience and walk back to your table after borrowing the cigar.

When you place the cigar on the outstretched fingers of your right hand, you will find it easy to grip the pin just below its head.

As long as you grip the pin in this way — between the second and third fingers of the right hand — you will find you can move your hand about freely. Don't rush; take your time with the moves.

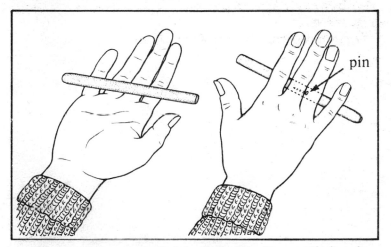

When you want to finish the trick, just pull the cigar upwards from your upturned right hand and let the pin fall on the floor whenever you wish. Remember to stand over a carpet and no one will spot the deception. Give the cigar a squeeze before handing it back to its owner; and this will close up the hole.

Three in a Row

What you do

Put three objects on a table. It doesn't matter what they are — they can be tumblers, books or coloured balls.

Place them in a straight line and invite someone to touch one of the three articles while your back is turned or while you are out of the room.

After he or she has done so, walk up to the objects, take the person's hand and ask him to think hard of the object he has touched.

Close your eyes and pretend to be picking up his thoughts. Open your eyes and at once touch the object he had previously selected.

This is a very baffling mystery to those not in the know and is one of the few tricks which you can repeat straight away without any fear of anyone spotting how it is done.

But don't do it more than two or three times and remember to make the most of the occasion. Pretend to think hard to convince your audience that it is not an easy trick to accomplish. In short — be a magician.

How you do it

Like many good tricks, this one requires the help of a friend. It should be an adult who smokes but could be a schoolfriend who doesn't.

Your secret assistant must be sitting or standing near the three objects so that you can see him or her as soon as you pretend to pick up the thoughts of the person who has touched one of the three objects.

If an adult is helping you, then he signals which object has been touched with a cigarette. If the cigarette is in the left-hand side of his mouth then you know it's the left-hand object *facing him* that has been touched.

If his cigarette is in the right-hand side of his mouth then it's the right-hand object that has been touched — again, *facing him*.

If the cigarette is in the middle of his mouth then it must be the middle object.

Sometimes, a smart alec may touch all three objects — or none at all. If this happens, your secret stooge keeps his cigarette away from his mouth entirely. You then announce that whoever was supposed to touch one of the objects just didn't carry out your instructions correctly and that you are unable to carry on with the experiment.

If you haven't the help of a friend who smokes, then get your secret assistant to touch his mouth with his forefinger. But remember, he must signal the touched object *facing him*.

Heads or Tails

What you do

Take a 10p coin from your pocket, spin it on a table a couple of times and then invite one of your audience to blindfold you.

Tell him to spin the coin in the same way as you have done and you will tell him whether it has come down heads or tails.

This is another trick that you can perform more than once — but don't overdo it. The secret of every good performer is to leave his audience wanting more — never give them too much.

If you want to build up this trick, have cotton wool placed over your eyes before the blindfold is applied. It will not make any difference to your ability to tell your audience on which side the coin finishes its spin.

How you do it

The secret is in the coin. Take a 10p piece and, with a sharp knife, make a small nick on the top edge of the coin so as to leave a little of the metal sticking out.

Spin the coin on a polished surface. You will find that when it falls on the edge with the nick underneath it makes a slightly different noise from when it falls with the nick on top.

In other words, it's the *sound* of the coin settling down which tells you whether it has come up heads or tails. Try this out a few times, and you'll be able to recognize the difference. If you can't distinguish between the two sounds make a larger nick on the edge of the coin.

Don't let anyone nick the coin afterwards or you'll be 10p out of pocket.

Think of a Number

What you do

This is an old schoolboy trick which is still effective. Try it out on a friend and, unless he knows the secret, he will remain baffled.

On the opposite page you will find two methods of obtaining the same result, so you can try the first method and then, as an encore, the second.

In each case you must be sure that your victim follows your instructions exactly. If necessary, supply him with a pencil and paper.

Warn him that you cannot guarantee success, but you have a feeling he has special powers which will help you to succeed.

However, if you're not much good at arithmetic yourself, then leave well alone.

How you do it

Tell your friend to think of a number — but not to tell you what it is. In this case let us imagine that the number is 5. Then you ask him to do the following without telling you the results.

Tell him to multiply the number by itself. He will then have 25.

Next he must take 1 from the number he originally had in his mind. Result: 4.

This, too, must be multiplied by itself, making 16.

He subtracts this sum (16) from his first total (25) and the result is 9.

Now tell him to add 1 to this total and this will give him 10. You then ask him what the final number is. You then halve this final total yourself and tell him his original number: 5.

Challenged to do it again, use this different method.

Tell your friend to multiply the number he thought of by 3. Let's assume he again thought of 5, so this gives you 15. Tell him to add 1 and this gives you 16. Instruct him to multiply this number by 3 and add the first number he thought of. The result will be 48 plus 5. Get him to tell you this final total. The result must always end with 3. Discard this yourself and announce that the number he originally had in his mind was the other one: 5.

The Travelling Cigarette Paper

What you do

Pick up a packet of do-it-yourself cigarette papers. Get your assistant to select three of these papers and screw each one into a tiny ball.

Pick up one of these pellets with your right hand and place it in the left hand. Clench the left hand with the paper inside it.

Now do exactly the same with the second screwed-up paper.

Finally, take the third little ball and either flick it into the fire or get someone to smoulder it into ashes with a cigarette.

That's the end of that, you say, but the strange part of this trick is that the third scrap of paper hasn't been destroyed at all. For here it is back with the other two.

Open the left hand to show that there are the three wisps of paper.

How you do it

The explanation is that when you first ask the member of your audience to screw up the cigarette papers you take the packet of papers and put it back in your pocket.

While your assistant is busy screwing up the paper, you take hold of another screwed-up cigarette paper which you had placed in this pocket beforehand.

You will find this move easier to do with your right hand if you are right-handed and with your left if you are left-handed. You may need a little practice, but it's not difficult.

Keep this extra wisp of paper hidden between the tips of your second and first finger. Then drop it into the left hand when you take the first piece of screwed-up paper from your helper.

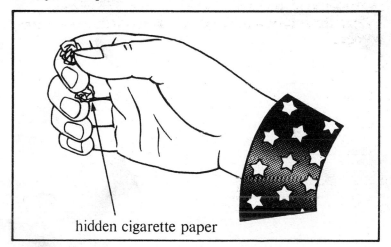

hidden cigarette paper

Add the second paper pellet. Now you have three screwed-up cigarette papers in the left hand.

Open the left hand at the end of the trick and you can show that instead of two little pellets you have three.

The Obedient Ball

What you do

The performer shows his audience a small ball through which a length of cord has been threaded.

He holds the cord at both ends with each hand but instead of the ball dropping smoothly down the cord, as you would expect, he orders it to stop and the ball at once remains stationary.

On the command 'Start,' the ball moves again down the cord. He can repeat this as many times as he likes.

Finally, he hands the ball to a member of his audience, but no one else can control the ball's downward flight. Only the magician can do it.

How you do it

This trick can be bought at any magic shop or, if you are a do-it-yourself expert, you can make it.

The secret is in the ball itself. It needs to be solid, quite heavy and hard enough for a hole to be drilled through it.

First drill a hole straight through the centre. Then drill a second hole, leading off from the first but rejoining it lower down (see illustration). Both holes must be wider than the cord used.

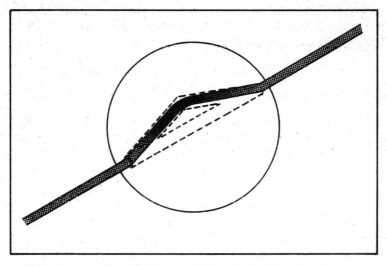

If you now thread the cord through the first hole, the ball will drop from the top to the bottom of the string when you hold an end in each hand.

But if you thread the string through the second hole, which is curved, then you will find you can control the downward movement of the ball merely by tightening the string. This is how you perform the trick.

Then, as if by accident, drop the ball so that it falls off the string. This will enable you to re-thread it before you hand it to one of the audience.

Finding an Object

What you do

Tell your audience that you are about to leave the room. While you are outside you want them to choose any object in the room and, on your return, you will be able to tell them which object they have chosen.

To achieve this, explain you need an assistant. Don't choose your assistant until you return — this will make it more magical.

On your return choose an assistant and ask him to point to a number of objects — without speaking to you — among which is the chosen object.

When he touches the appropriate item you will immediately be able to name the chosen object.

How you do it

The explanation is, of course, that you use a code.

The code you use is a matter for you to decide but a very simple one to remember uses the colours of the Union Jack.

Your friend first points to a number of objects before touching the right one. Then, just before he touches the selected item, he touches something coloured red. The next item he touches will be the correct one.

You can repeat the procedure, but the next time the code colour will be blue; the third time round the colour will be white. If you wanted to continue, then your assistant starts with red again.

As red, white and blue are easy to remember, you will have no difficulty in knowing that the article touched immediately after one of these colours is the right one.

Golly! My whiskers are white I'm not having those touched. I'm off!

Pick a Penny

What you do

Take four pennies and have someone in your audience
select one of the coins. Get him or her to note the date or
even to make a secret mark on the coin.

The coin is then placed on its own. The young performer
holds the other pennies in his hands and talks of the mystic
skills of the Orient, the Power of Thought or some such
misleading chat. The longer he talks the better but, of
course, he should not talk so long that the audience
becomes restless.

Then, turning his head away, the magician invites the
person who chose the penny to drop the coin into his
hands with the others.

Closing his eyes, he places each coin in turn against his
forehead. In this way he selects the chosen coin.

How you do it

All that you have to ensure is that after the coin has been
selected it is placed on its own on a table or shelf so that no
one touches it until it is handed to you.

This enables the coin to cool down so that it can be
easily identified when placed on your forehead.

While you are chatting, the coins held in your hands get
quite warm, thereby making it easy to recognize the cold
coin when it is returned and placed among the warm coins.

You can have some fun with this, especially if you say
that you will now attempt an experiment in Uri Gellerism.

*Better not tell Uri
what you're up to!*

The Uri Geller Coin

What you do

You should perform this on top of a white table cloth or a piece of black velvet.

Produce half-a-dozen pillbox lids and place them in a row.

Put a 2p piece on the table, turn your back and invite someone to cover the coin with one of the pillbox lids.

When this has been done, turn around and slowly pass your hand, palm downturned, across the top of each cover.

Move slowly up and down — just as Uri Geller does on TV — and, finally, come to rest and touch one of the covers.

Take it off — and there is the 2p piece.

How you do it

You have secretly stuck a black or brown hair to the rim of the coin you use. The hair must be just long enough to jut out from under the cover when the coin is placed beneath it.

On a white tablecloth you can easily see the hair, but don't try to do this trick more than once to the same audience. You can use this principle with other objects, but a coin seems to work best.

Of course, if you want to work this trick on the black velvet of your magician's table you will need to stick a white or grey hair to the coin.

You're not getting any of <u>my</u> white hairs— try grandma!

The Karate Pencil Chop

What you do

This is by no means a new trick, but is very slick and effective. As a beginner in magic, you will find it useful if you are suddenly called upon to demonstrate your new skills.

All you will need is a long, slim pencil and a borrowed £1 note.

Tell your audience that it is sometimes possible to fold a pound note so that it has an edge as sharp as a razor. Ask someone to hold the pencil *firmly at each end* and then you fold the note lengthways.

Make two moves to cut the pencil in half and at the third attempt succeed; the pencil is split, and your helper is left holding the two ends.

How you do it

The secret has nothing whatever to do with either the pencil or the pound note.

What you do is to stick your forefinger out alongside the edge of the pound note as you bring the note down and withdraw it just as quickly after your *finger* has split the pencil in two.

Do it quickly and no one will spot what you have done.

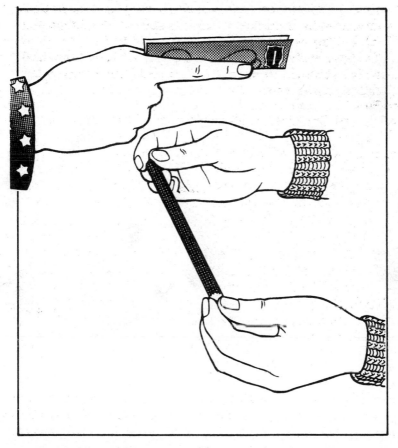

The Prediction Dice

What you do

This won't fool professional dice throwers, but the young magician isn't likely to have any of these in his audience in the early stages of his magical career.

Begin by writing something on a piece of paper, then inform your audience that you have made a prediction of something which will happen in the immediate future.

Put your prediction in an envelope, seal it and give it to someone for safe keeping.

Now invite someone else to throw three dice.

Next, ask him to pick up each dice, add the top and bottom number together and give you the total sum produced by all three dice.

Have the sealed envelope opened. The audience will be astonished when your assistant reads out *'I PREDICT THE SUM THROWN BY THE DICE WILL TOTAL 21.'*

How you do it

First (to save time) before your performance write on the paper, *'I PREDICT THE SUM THROWN BY THE DICE WILL TOTAL   '*. Leave a space so that you can add the amount in front of your audience.

Now, as any dice thrower knows, the top and bottom number of any single dice thrown will always add up to seven. If you throw two dice, the number will be 14. If it's three, then the number is 21 and so on.

Note that your prediction does not foretell the top numbers thrown, just the total of the top and bottom numbers. No one is likely to spot this.

Again, this is a trick you do only once. By the time someone has almost worked out how you achieved such a miracle you have moved on to another trick and his concentration is elsewhere.

A real Seven-Up trick—every time.

The Vanishing Coin

What you do

Coin tricks are always popular. This one is clean cut and will mystify most people, especially if you follow it up immediately with the coin trick which follows.

Borrow a 5p piece and get a friend to put a mark on it. Now hold it in your left hand and place a handkerchief over it. Let your friend feel the coin through the material, keeping the handkerchief over your left hand.

Count aloud, 'One — Two — Three — GO' and, on the word 'Go' whisk the handkerchief away with your right hand. The coin has vanished.

You now reach into your pocket and produce the vanished coin — with your friend's mark still on it.

How you do it

The secret here is in your handkerchief. You have to stitch a 5p piece into the hem. If the hem isn't big enough, you will need two handkerchiefs sewn together with the hidden 5p piece in turn sewn into a small secret bag between the two handkerchiefs. Coloured hankies are best.

This is the coin your friend feels through the material — the marked one remains hidden in your right hand while he does so. You put the marked coin in your pocket at the same time as you flick the handkerchief upwards with your left hand to show that it is empty.

Make the most of this vanish — it's a good one.

Coin in Water Vanish

What you do

This trick makes a good follow-up to the previous one in which you made a 5p piece vanish.

Tell your audience that this particular 5p piece obviously has some remarkable travelling powers and that you would like to try a second experiment with it.

This time take a glass full of water and again put your friend's coin in the handkerchief as you did before.

Hold the handkerchief with the coin inside over the glass of water so that the glass is completely covered and invite one of your audience to feel it and then to listen carefully.

Sure enough, the person will hear a little tinkle of something falling into the glass. For an added twist you can even let him hold the coin and let it go when you tell him.

Once more, when you whisk the handkerchief away from the glass of water, the coin will have vanished and there will be nothing but water in the glass.

This time, for a variation, cut open a lemon and there inside lies the marked coin. You should get some applause for all this.

How you do it

You need a glass disc the size of a 5p piece for this clever vanish. Any glass merchant will cut you one, but make sure he also smooths the edge for you.

Use any handkerchief and fold it around the glass disc — hidden beforehand in your left hand. It is this disc that your friend feels through the material and thinks is the marked coin.

When the glass disc falls into the water, it will make a slight noise but when you hold the glass up your audience will see only water in the tumbler.

Your right hand still holds the marked coin. On your tablecloth have a lemon with a small slit already cut in the side away from the audience. You will find it easy enough to slide the marked coin gently into the slit as you pick up the lemon. Give it a push with your thumb and it will go deeper into the fruit.

Put the lemon on a plate and, using a fruit knife, just cut it open.

The Sinking Disc

What you do

Take a tumbler and a glass jug. Partly fill the jug with water. Show the tumbler to be free of any preparation by rattling your magic wand inside the glass. Pour water into the glass.

Pick up a small metal disc about the size of a 5p piece, place it on top of the water and say the magic words 'Magick; Magick; Float.' The disc will now float on top of the water.

Take the floating disc from the water. Let your audience examine it and replace it on the water. This time say, 'Magick; Magick; Sink,' but say it *before* you replace the disc on the water as it will sink immediately.

This is a quick, simple opening trick for your first magical performance. However, you will need to practise to ensure that you don't give away the secret.

Remember, as with every trick, it is the presentation that counts. If you are able to tell a story about the disc having special magical powers known only to you and that you alone can make it float or sink at will, then you are at once turning a simple party trick into a truly magical event.

The fact that you alone can command the disc to float or sink is in itself a magical achievement. And this is what makes a magician different from everyone else.

As a variation, you can first make the disc float yourself and challenge anyone to do the same. But when they try, they will always fail.

How you do it

Two discs identical in appearance are used.

The floating disc is made of aluminium, the sinking disc of tin. You need discs about the size of a 5p piece, and your local garage, metal merchant or hardware store should be able to supply you with these. Or, if you have a friend who is a do-it-yourself enthusiast, ask him to help.

Paint both discs the same colour, and you are ready to baffle your audience. Start with the aluminium disc, keeping the other hidden in your right hand. When the sinking disc is needed just switch one for the other.

If you find this too difficult, have the tin disc on your magician's table before you start, hidden by a silk handkerchief.

Place the aluminium disc beside the tin one after you have floated it and proceed to explain its magical powers. Move the handkerchief to hide it and then pick up the tin disc when you have finished talking.

I've heard of the sinking pound but this is ridiculous!

37

The Magnetized Wand

What you do

This is something you can do at any time during your show.

Just pick up your wand, rub it briskly on your coat sleeve and remark that as it now appears to be fully magnetized you will attempt to suspend it from your finger tips.

Then, with your left hand, take the wand at one end and place it at the tips of the fingers of your right hand. Take your left hand away and it remains suspended.

Although not a great trick in itself, it creates an amusing effect which can help to establish your reputation as a person of mystery.

How you do it

There are two ways to achieve this effect. One is to apply a very weak solution of glue and water to your fingers — just a dab on each finger.

When this dries, you will find it provides a sticky enough surface to allow the wand to cling to your fingers.

The other method is the special way in which you first grip the wand. Put the tip of your little finger and the tip of

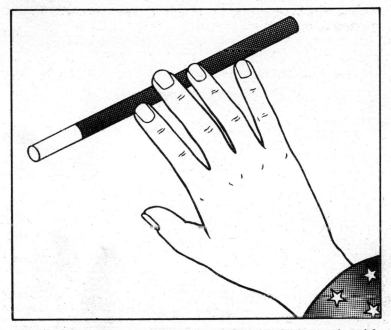

your forefinger against the side of the wand, then grip with the middle two fingers.

With a little practice you will find that you can actually hold the wand in this manner, with fingers outstretched. Invite someone to take the wand away from your fingers and the audience still won't be able to spot your secret.

The Restored Cigarette

What you do

This is a twist on a very old trick. In the original, a matchstick is used; for my up-to-date version, use a cigarette.

Spread out a white handkerchief on a table and, borrowing a cigarette, place it in the centre. Get the person who loaned you the cigarette to mark it in some way with a felt pen so that he will recognize it again. A small ink blob will do.

Fold the corners of the handkerchief to cover the cigarette and then fold the handkerchief again so that the cigarette is completely covered.

Ask the cigarette lender if he can feel it between the folds of the handkerchief.

Then take the handkerchief with the cigarette still inside and get someone to break the cigarette into several pieces. When this has been done, take it back to the lender and get him to confirm that it has been well and truly broken.

You should get some laughs here, especially in view of the high cost of cigarettes.

Shake the handkerchief above the table and the cigarette, now intact, will fall out.

Give it to its owner, and he will have to agree that his original mark is still on the cigarette paper!

How you do it

You first need a hem-stitched white handkerchief. Put a cigarette secretly into the hem beforehand, if necessary stitch in with large stitches, and make sure that when you fold the corners you place this corner just in front of the marked cigarette lying on the handkerchief.

Pick up the handkerchief and, in doing so, offer the cigarette in the hem to your assistant. This is the one he breaks into pieces, but because it is hidden in the hem it

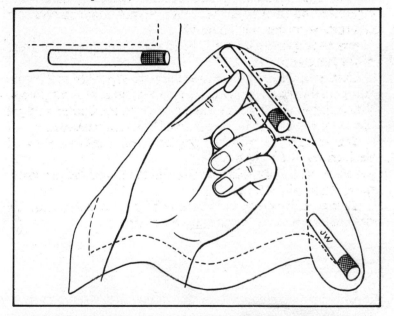

remains there when you shake out the handkerchief at the end of the trick. The marked cigarette should fall into the folds of the held handkerchief.

It is the marked cigarette which falls clear — magically restored!

You can achieve exactly the same effect with a wooden match, but I prefer this new cigarette version.

Two's Company

What you do

Most magicians like to include a card trick in their performance. Here is an easy one which will astonish most people who don't know the secret.

Give a member of the audience two cards — let's say they are the seven of diamonds and the eight of hearts.

Get him or her to place the cards in different positions in the pack.

Take the pack, face downwards, firmly between the thumb and forefinger of the right hand. Give the pack a swift jerk and throw all the cards on the floor . . . except two.

Turn these two cards over and show your audience that you have retained the two original cards.

How you do it

This is a case of things being not quite what they seem.

The cards you give to your audience are *not* the same as those you produce at the end of the trick, although few, if any, of your audience will spot this.

The cards you gave out were the seven of diamonds and the eight of hearts, but the cards you retained in your hand after throwing the pack on the floor were the eight of diamonds and the seven of hearts.

You had placed one card at the top and one at the bottom of the deck before you started the trick. When you throw the cards on the floor, you will find it easy enough to keep these two cards between your thumb and forefinger.

Keep them face downwards for a moment before turning them upwards.

Always pick two cards of the same colour for this neat little trick. Also, the cards must follow each other in value, i.e., a five and a six or a three and a four.

The Uri Geller Banana

What you do

Take a banana in your left hand, remarking that it is sometimes possible to make the fruit split into three or four parts just by thinking hard and by touching the skin with a fruit knife.

Point out that Uri Geller claims to have similar powers and that you will now try to do the same.

Holding the banana upright, circle the skin in three sections with the tip of the knife touching the skin lightly — don't cut it.

Put down the knife and peel the fruit. Your audience will be astonished to see the banana break into three pieces just as you predicted, yet, the outside skin is still intact and uncut.

How you do it

Before facing your audience you take a banana and go to work on it with a needle and thread. See illustration. Pass the needle through one side of the fruit, leaving a long bit of thread hanging outside. Push through point 2. Using the same hole, insert the needle into the banana again, and push through to point 3. Carry on in the same way until you have sewn right round so that the needle is brought out through the same hole through which it entered

the banana. Leave another long bit of thread loose when you arrive back at the starting point.

You will now have threaded the piece of cotton all around the banana directly under the skin. Take the two ends of the thread and draw them together, cutting the inside of the banana. Cut in this way in two places, the banana will collapse into three pieces when peeled.

The holes made by the needle are so small that no one will spot them. This is a good party trick, especially if you manage to add your specially prepared banana to a bowl of fruit beforehand.

Telling the Age

What you do

Invite someone to think his or her age — it can be anyone up to 60 years old — but not to tell it to you.

Then hand them six cards on which you have written 180 different numbers, 30 on each card.

Tell him to look at each card and then to place in one pile the cards giving his age. In another pile he places the cards from which his age is missing.

The performer takes the pile of cards giving the age and at once tells the person how old he or she is.

How you do it

First copy out the numbers on the squares exactly (see illustration) on white paper and paste them on to pieces of cardboard.

The trick now works itself. The age can easily be found by adding together the number in the upper right-hand corner of each card.

For example, if 5 is the age of your friend, he will select the cards with 1 and 4 in the top right-hand corner.

If the number of years is 60, he will pick the cards with 4, 8, 16 and 32.

If you are good at maths, you will soon be able to work out the addition with just a quick glance at the cards.

Remember, *don't* appear to be adding anything up. The quicker you give the right number of years, the better.

3	6	7	10	11	2
14	15	18	19	22	23
26	27	30	31	34	35
38	39	42	43	46	47
50	51	54	55	58	59

5	6	7	13	12	4
14	15	20	21	22	23
28	29	30	31	36	37
52	38	39	44	45	46
47	53	54	55	60	13

9	10	11	12	13	8
14	15	24	25	26	27
28	29	30	31	40	41
42	43	44	45	46	47
56	57	58	59	60	13

3	5	7	9	11	1
13	15	17	19	21	23
25	27	29	31	33	35
37	39	41	43	45	47
49	51	53	55	57	59

17	18	19	20	21	16
22	23	24	25	26	27
28	29	30	31	48	49
50	51	52	53	54	55
56	57	58	59	30	60

33	34	35	36	37	32
38	39	40	41	42	43
44	45	46	47	48	49
50	51	52	53	54	55
56	57	58	59	60	41

The Kojak Card Trick

What you do

No book on magic for beginners would be complete without this great card trick. It is easy to do; no sleight of hand is involved, but the effect is truly magical.

The magician shows the four jacks — one above the other. Then he tells the story of four New York crooks being pursued to a warehouse. He places the four knaves on the top of the pack. Using the rest of the pack as the warehouse, he explains that three of the gangsters went to explore the different floors of the building, while the fourth remained as a look-out.

He then puts one knave on the table — face upwards — and places the other three — face downwards — in different parts of the pack. He explains that the look-out sees Kojak and his team of New York cops approaching, so he calls to the other three to come up to the roof of the warehouse.

The magician flips the pack three times, turns over the top three cards and there, unbelievably, are the three jacks.

How you do it

This modernized version of the old *Robbers and Soldiers* trick is very easy to perform.

The three jacks were not placed in different parts of the pack although they seemed to be. The performer has seven cards in his hand — not four.

Between the first jack and the second jack are three other secret cards. Any three will do as the audience does not see their faces.

They are so placed that the audience cannot see them (illustration 1).

If the magician were to spread out the cards (which, of course, he would never do), they would appear as in illustration 2.

It is the three extra secret cards which go into different parts of the pack.

Without doubt, this is the greatest card trick for any beginner.

The Spinning 10p

What you do

This is a puzzling little trick and is useful if ever you are called upon to do some close-up magic.

Put a borrowed 10p piece, edge upwards, on a shiny surface and place the forefinger of your left hand on top to keep it in position.

Keep your other fingers and thumb bunched together and rub the top of the outstretched forefinger with the forefinger of your other hand.

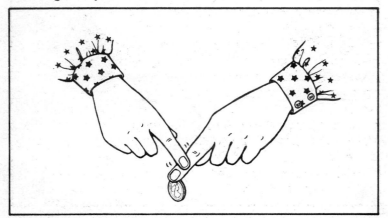

Suddenly, the coin spins as if by the gentle massage of one finger against the other.

How you do it

Of course it isn't the actions of the right finger on top of the other which makes the coin spin, even though it appears that way.

The explanation is that, after stroking your left forefinger in this way, you jerk out your right thumb with a swift movement. It is the thumb of your right hand —

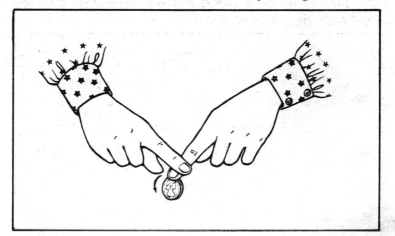

hidden by your right forefinger — which hits against the coin and makes it spin. This trick works best on a not too smooth surface.

A Colour Change

What you do

Take a long, red coloured pencil and roll it in a sheet of newspaper. Leave the lead point of the pencil peeping out.

Now push out the pencil from the other end. It has turned into a pencil of an entirely different colour. Screw up the newspaper and you will have the audience puzzled.

You could achieve the same effect with a stick or with your own magic wand.

How you do it

Again, things aren't what they seem. The red coloured stick or pencil is really a white one throughout.

To make it appear red at the start of the trick, paste a red paper tube round it. When you draw the pencil from the sheet of rolled up paper this red paper tube will remain hidden inside the sheet of paper. Grip the pencil hard through the paper to ensure that this happens.

After removing the pencil, toss the paper aside, and it will indeed seem as though the pencil has changed its colour.

That's the last time I'm going in the Tube. I don't want _my_ colour changed!

The Coloured Silks

What you do

Show your audience four small envelopes and four silk handkerchiefs of different colours. Ask a member of the audience to examine them. Then turn away while someone puts a coloured silk into each envelope. Ask her or him to mix up the envelopes and to put them in your hands while your back is still turned. Then you turn around, and one by one you bring forward the envelopes and name the silk inside each one. Give each envelope to a different person as you name them and ask that each person should remember the colour given to him.

Now get each person to name the colour of his or her silk and to open the envelope. They will find that you have correctly named the colour inside each of the four sealed envelopes.

How you do it

You need jeans with two hip pockets in them, and a second set of both the coloured silk handkerchiefs and the envelopes.

Place the handkerchiefs from one of the sets into each of your second set of envelopes. Seal these envelopes and put them into the *right-hand* pocket, having arranged them in an easy-to-remember order. A simple order to memorize would be red, white and blue, with another colour such as green or yellow as the fourth colour.

Make sure no one is behind you at the start of this effect, for all you do is to put the first four envelopes in your left-hand hip pocket and take out those on the right-hand side. This easy move will be hidden by your jacket.

I'll buy some jeans tomorrow!

Sand and Water

What you do

Show your friends a glass bowl; pour in some water and some sand from a paper bag.

Put your hand in the water and stir it around to show that it is indeed a muddy mixture. Tell your audience to imagine that this is sand at the bottom of the sea.

Announce that you have special powers which enable you to produce dry sand from the sea bed and, although you don't propose to take them to the bottom of the ocean to prove this, you will be prepared to demonstrate these powers by using the sand in the glass bowl.

Again, put your hand in the sand which has now settled at the bottom of the bowl, take it out and hold it above a saucer. A fine cascade of dry sand will fall from your clenched fist.

Repeat this several times and accept the congratulations.

How you do it

To prepare for this sand and water trick you must first make a few tiny bags out of waterproof paper.

Cut out two pieces of this paper about 2-3cm square and stick three of the edges of each together to make one of the bags you will need. Make two or three bags. Put some teaspoonsfuls of dry sand into the bag and using colourless glue, seal its remaining open side. You are all set.

These bags of dry sand are hidden in the same sand that you pour into the water from your paper bag. Just pull the bags out, one at a time, and squeeze them, and the dry sand will run from your clenched fist.

Screw the paper up tightly in each case, and you can put it back into the sand in the bowl without anyone spotting what you have done.

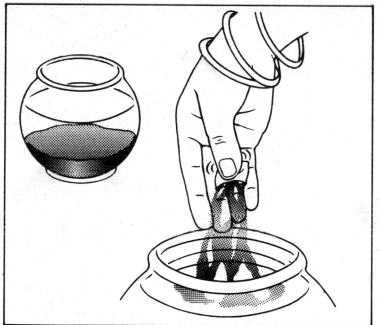

The Mysterious Message

What you do

For this effect you will need two writing slates, a slate pencil or a piece of white chalk (or two pieces of cardboard and a felt tip pen) and a 2cm wide length of coloured ribbon.

Place the slates or cardboard pieces on top of each other and tie them in a parcel with the ribbon. Leave the ribbon in a bow so that it can be easily untied.

Invite two members of the audience to write their initials on the outside of each slate. Untie the bow, turn the slates over and get them to write their initials again. Thus, each side of each slate will have been initialled.

Tie the slates together again, draw the attention of the audience to what has happened and point out that the two sides of each slate were free of writing when you began the effect.

Now have someone untie the slates again. To everyone's surprise, your audience will find a message inside the package, and it will be written right across the face of one of the initialled slates.

How you do it

This effect is achieved by simply writing the message in letters not more than 2cm high on the face of one of the slates before your performance begins.

The ribbon hides the writing, and you start with the hidden message on the outside of one of the slates. Turn the slates over carefully and your message will now be on the inside.

You can mention that you have the slates tied in this way to prevent anyone tampering with them, and the fact that you have had each side of each slate initialled will persuade the audience that the arrival of the writing must have been achieved by some strange magical power.

If you have a friend whom you can trust, get him to take a pack of cards before you begin. Let him hold the pack and take out any card he chooses. Ask him to remember the card and then put it back in the pack.

All you have to do is to write the name of *any card* on the slate beforehand. Then, when the secret writing is revealed and the name of the card shown to the audience, ask your friend if that was the card he picked. He agrees that it was, and you have achieved yet another magical mystery.

A Slate Trick

What you do

Here is another slate trick which you can perform immediately after the previous one.

Take one of the slates, show that it is clean on both sides and — to impress this fact on your audience — wipe it with a small damp sponge.

Now invite someone to select any number between one and five. Then tear out a page from a newspaper and wrap it around the slate.

Hand the package to one of your friends and ask him to sit on it.

Count aloud to whatever number has been chosen and invite your friend to look at the slate.

There, on the face of the slate, the audience will see the chosen number written in white chalk.

How you do it

Before you begin performing this trick, in mirror-writing write with thick chalk on each of the first few pages of a newspaper the numbers one to five. But put the numbers on the back of the pages, not the front.

Thus, page two has the number one written on it; page four has two and so on. By writing these numbers on the

back of page one and on the *back* of page three, your audience will not be able to see them.

You have only to remember on which pages you have written your five numbers and to make sure that the side of the paper with the required number is the side facing the slate when you wrap up your parcel.

When your friend sits on the slate, his weight will be sufficient to leave an imprint of the number on the slate.

Show the slate to your audience, crumple up the newspaper and you have brought off yet another mystery for them to wonder about.

Pick a View

What you do

Show the audience about half-a-dozen picture postcards. Each picture must be different, but all must be of famous beauty spots or places with which the audience will be familiar.

Return the postcards to your table, and then invite the audience to call out the names of some of the places they have seen. As the places are named, write each one on a slip of paper. Fold the pieces of paper as you proceed and put each into a hat.

When you have done this, take the postcards into the audience and ask someone to select a card. Offer them face downwards so that neither you nor he knows which view has been selected.

Now give the hat to someone else and invite him to take out one of the pieces of paper, unfold the slip and call out the place he has selected.

It will be the same as the view on the chosen postcard.

How you do it

For a start, the packet of postcards from which a member of your audience selects a view is not the same package as the one you showed originally.

You use a different pack with the same view on each card — this view is identical to one of the views in the first pack. This pack is on your table, hidden by that very useful silk handkerchief. You exchange the original packet of postcards for the fake packet when you first return to your table.

You must also ignore the places called out by the audience and just put down whatever is the view appearing on the packet of all-alike postcards. No one will know you are doing this but be sure to take the hat away as soon as he has selected a slip, otherwise he might try and catch you out by picking up a second slip immediately afterwards.

Remember, too, not to write on any more slips than the number of postcards in each packet.

Your House and Age

What you do

This is another mathematical trick — more fun with a pocket calculator but still effective without one.

Ask a friend if his house or flat has a number and if he is prepared to tell the truth about his age. If the answer in both cases is Yes then proceed as follows.

Instruct him to carry out the following without telling you any of the results. Tell him to write down the number on the door of his home. Then he must double it and add 5. He next multiplies by 50 and adds his age. Now he adds the number of days in a year (365) and, finally, subtracts the original number of Members of Parliament (615).

Get him to tell you the final result, and you can then immediately tell him not only the number on his front door but also his age.

How you do it

This is a self-working effect which will go down well with any audience.

The final total will give you your figures. The first two figures will be the number of your friend's house and the second two will be his or her age.

If your friend's door is numbered below 10 then it will be the first figure only that indicates the number. If the house number is in three figures then the final figure will consist of five figures, and the first three numbers will be the number.

Just one more point: 366 will have to be added if it is a leap year. To compensate for this, tell your friend to add four instead of five when you give him his third instruction.

I'm still figuring it out!

A Word in a Million

What you do

This is a clever mathematical trick involving the discovery of a word in a book. It looks great if you use a pocket calculator.

Hand someone a book either with less than 100 pages or, if there are more than 100 pages, tell him to select any page in the first one hundred. Now tell him to select any word in the first nine lines of that page and also ensure that it is one of the first nine words on that line.

Instruct him to carry out the following without telling you any of the results. Ask him to put a mark on the word and then to close the book. You will attempt to find out the word by your skill as a mathematician. He will probably need a pencil and paper to carry out your instructions, so have them handy, just in case. If you have a pocket calculator, better still, just hand it to him.

First tell him to double the number of pages, then multiply the answer by 5. He adds 20 to this amount. Next, he adds the number of the line. Then he adds 5 and multiplies by 10. Now he adds the number of the word in the line and subtracts 250 from the final total.

Ask him to tell you the final result — or hand you the calculator.

Look at it for a moment. Pick up the book and turn to the selected word.

How you do it

This trick is best described by using an actual word in this book as an example.

Let us suppose page 86 has been chosen. The member of your audience has then selected line six and the third word which happens to be *instructions*. Now ask him to do the following — without telling you any results till the final one.

Tell him to double the number of the page	172
Multiply the answer by 5	860
Add 20 to this amount	880
Now add the number of the line (in this case 6)	886
Add 5	891
Multiply by 10	8910
Add the number of the word in the line (in this case 3)	8913
Subtract 250	8663

Ask to be told the final figure which, in this case is 8663. This at once tells you the page is 86; the line is the sixth and the chosen word is the third on that line.

Turn to the appropriate page and announce the word — *instructions*.

Use any book you like *except Ali Cat's Magic Circle Book of Tricks*.

The Flying Ring

What you do

Borrow a wedding ring and hold it in your left hand between thumb and forefinger. Cover the ring with a handkerchief held in your right hand and give it to a spectator to hold, after twisting the handkerchief round the ring so that he firmly holds the ring through the material.

Tell your audience that you are about to perform a classic act of magic, and that you will cause the ring to fly through space at your command.

With your assistant still holding the ring through the handkerchief just take one corner and whisk it from his grasp. Show both sides of the handkerchief.

The ring will have vanished.

Now show both hands empty and then reach out and produce the ring at your finger tips. Bow to your applause.

This is not a trick for you to try straightaway, but it will pay you to practise it as you become more skilled.

How you do it

The principle of this trick is the same as that of the broken and restored cigarette.

Prepare the handkerchief either by sewing a cheap wedding ring into a small pocket in one corner or by stitching it into the hem if it is wide enough. See the illustration on page 33 — the principle is the same.

This is the ring the spectator holds; you take the original ring away, hidden in your left hand, after arranging the handkerchief for him.

To show both hands empty, i.e., without the ring, you will need a small hook hidden conveniently on your clothes.

Make the hook out of a piece of wire and have it placed to the rear of your jeans pocket on the left leg where it will

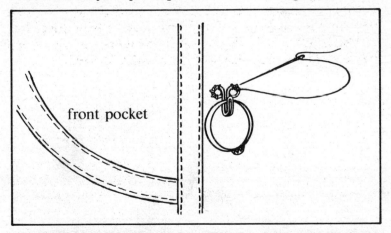

front pocket

remain hidden by your jacket. Slip the ring on to the hook during the trick. The hook can be sewn in permanently or just fixed temporarily for the occasion.

Once the ring is hidden you can show both hands to be empty. To produce the ring, stand sideways to the audience with your right side facing them.

Take the ring from its secret hiding place with your left hand and, with a flourish, produce it at your finger tips.

The Uncanny Ash

What you do

This is a more advanced trick. Properly presented, it will baffle most adults.

Wait until you spot a fairly full ashtray and then announce you will attempt an experiment in the Power of Thought.

Take a little of the ash and put it in a clean ashtray. Then invite someone to help you. Tell him or her to sit down facing you and to put his hands in the same position as yours: palm downwards, thumbs touching, fingers close together.

Pick up some ash and rub it on the back of his right hand. Tell him to follow your movements, which are to pass his right hand slowly over the top of his left hand, and then to return both hands to their original position. Go through these motions yourself to show him what to do. Then get him to do the same.

Now invite him to turn over his left hand. He will find a clear ash mark on the palm of this hand.

In other words, the ash from the back of the *right* hand has travelled downwards through space to leave its mark on the palm of the *left* hand.

Uncanny.

How you do it

The secret is subtle, and clever. When you first arrange the ash in the second ashtray, you leave a small amount sticking to the tip of the middle finger of your right hand. Make sure it is underneath where it can't be seen. Put none on the tip.

Then, pretending to arrange your friend's hands in the right position, you gently press this ash against the palm of his left hand.

After this move, take as long as you like to openly put some ash on the back of his right hand and to have him carry out the movements that follow. Don't hurry.

By the time he has finished and sees the ash which has mysteriously arrived on the palm of his left hand, which has been turned face downwards throughout, he will swear that you never touched him there at all.

Again, don't hurry any of this. The longer you take — after secretly planting the ash on his palm — the more effective the final pay-off.

The Uncanny Ash is a reputation builder for any young magician. Try it and see.

Water into Wine

What you do

Take a glass jug of water and pour the contents into four glasses in the following manner.

First, pour some water into glass 1. Nothing happens.

Second, pour some water into glass 2 and it will turn red.

Third, pour some water into glass 3 and it remains uncoloured.

Fourth, pour some water into glass 4 and it will turn red.

Now mix the contents of glass 1 with the contents of glass 2 and the liquid becomes red.

Pour this back into the water left in the jug and that too turns red.

Mix the contents of glasses 3 and 4 and the water becomes clear.

Finally, pour this back into the glass jug and the water is now clear once more.

You are left as you begin: with a jug of clear water and four empty glasses.

How you do it

This is a self-working effect. All you need are some chemicals, obtainable from your local chemist or school laboratory. Your science master will be able to advise you.

First put a teaspoonful of liquor potassae in the water in the jug.

Second, put three drops of phenol pthaleine (dissolved in alcohol) in glass 2.

Glass 3 is prepared with a small pinch of tartaric acid, in powder form, in its base.

Glass 4 (as with glass 2) has three drops of phenol pthaleine at the bottom.

Follow the moves outlined and you will find the water will turn red and then clear just as I have described.

Don't drink it—you might get tummy ache!

The Coded Pack

What you do

You are now about to tackle some of the great card tricks of all time.

No sleight of hand is involved, but you should by now be sufficiently skilled to present these baffling effects.

You can have a bunch of cards taken from the pack and held by a member of the audience. Although you haven't touched the cards in any way, you can at once tell him every card he is holding.

Or you can have three cards placed in a sealed envelope. Take another pack, select three cards yourself and have them placed in another sealed envelope. Have each envelope initialled, exchange them and, when they are slit open, the cards, your audience will find, are identical.

There are many other tricks you can perform in this manner but, as always, remember that it is your own presentation which will ensure success.

The secret is on the opposite page. Once you have understood how it works you will be able to work out many similar tricks for yourself.

How you do it

An ordinary pack of cards is used, but they are arranged beforehand in a special order. Providing the pack is *never* shuffled and only cut, the pack will always remain in the pre-arranged order.

There are several ways of pre-arranging a pack, but one of the easiest to remember is based on the sentence 'Eight kings threatened to save nine fair ladies for one sick knave.'

The pack should be arranged in the order of Diamonds; Clubs; Hearts and Spades. The code itself is Eight (eight); kings (king): threatened (three, ten); to (two); save (seven); nine (nine); fair (five); ladies (queen); for (four); one (Ace); sick (six); knave (jack). See illustrations page 78.

All you have to do is to memorize the sentence and to remember the order of the suits. Arrange your pack in this order and you will be able to perform some astonishing card feats.

By just glancing at the card above those taken, you know at once the card, or cards, taken by the other person.

Just repeat in your mind the sequence of the cards *beneath* this key card and then name them aloud as you remember them. It's that easy. For example, if the ten of clubs is the key card then you know the next card taken beneath the ten of clubs will be the two of hearts, then the seven of spades, then the nine of diamonds and so on.

In this manner, your pre-arranged pack will enable you to know the identity of every card selected by your audience — just one or a whole bunch.

Take your time. Don't hurry. The longer you appear to contemplate, the more difficult your task will appear to be to your audience. As ever though, don't ponder so long that they become restless.

Some magicians name every card in the pack — after it has been cut. A seemingly impossible feat. Now you can do the same.

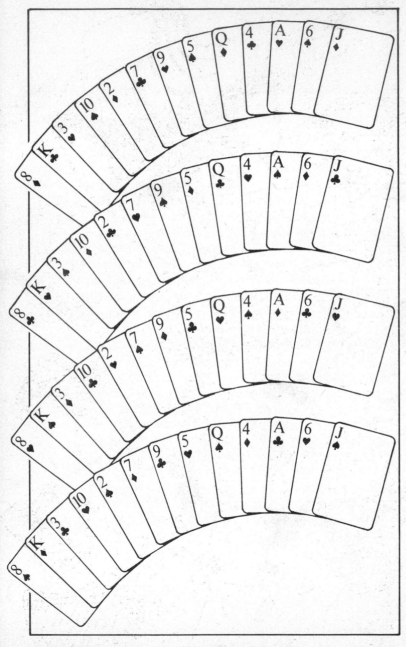

The Magic Book

What you do

Tell your audience how you went into a stationers' to buy a book on motor cars.

'The assistant said he had none in stock, but just as I was leaving I noticed this book on the shelf with a picture of a motor car on its front cover. The assistant was unwilling to sell it to me, because he said it wasn't really a book on cars; something had gone wrong in the printing, and as a result it was all blank pages.'

You then show your book is indeed nothing but blank pages.

'I asked why he kept the book, and he said the strange thing was that every so often he looked through the book and he did find pictures of motor cars — like that.'

And you show the blank pages are indeed covered with pictures of cars.

'I told him I thought this was very odd, and he said it was even odder than I thought because sometimes he looked through the book and found no pictures of motor cars at all — instead there were pictures of animals.'

At this point, you show the pages are covered with pictures of animals.

'That's all right,' I told the assistant. 'I'm very fond of animals as well. I'll take it.'

'Well,' said the assistant, 'you can have the book if you like, but remember — it is a magic book, and when you show it to anyone you may well find that it has gone back to blank pages again — as it has now.'

You now show that all the pages are blank once more.

How you do it

You need to buy a scrap book with thick paper, the thicker the better. You will find one in a major chain store. First use the same illustration for the two covers — one the same side up as the following illustrated pages and the cover of the blank book upside down.

Turn over about six pages and paste in a picture of a motor car. Turn over a further six pages and do the same again. Carry on until you have filled every sixth page in this manner. Finally, paste a slip of paper at the top right-hand edge on each page where there is a picture of a car.

Take the book again and paste on each page *before* the motor cars, pictures of animals. Continue until you have filled the book. This time paste a slip of paper at the bottom right-hand edge of the pages on which you have pasted a picture of an animal.

Now, if you hold the book in your left hand and flip through the pages with your right thumb at the top of the book, your audience will see pictures of motor cars. If your thumb is at the bottom, they will see pictures of animals.

Finally, turn the book upside down, run through it a third time and you will see only blank pages.

This is a neat trick and well worth the preparation. If you are clever with a paint brush, you can make your own pictures. The contrast then could be between flowers and birds or whatever interests you.

But don't forget that the back of each page must be left blank, otherwise you won't be able to show blank pages to everyone at the start and at the finish of your performance.

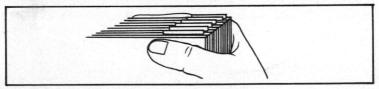

The Torn Cigarette Paper

What you do

This is for the more advanced performer, not because it is difficult but because it requires some practice and dexterity.

Take a cigarette paper from a packet of papers, tear it into pieces and then roll the bits into a ball.

Unroll the ball and show that all the pieces have mysteriously become rejoined.

Properly done, this is a reputation builder, and your friends will talk about this simple but mystifying effect long after other tricks have been forgotten.

How you do it

The easiest way to achieve this effect is to have a small ball of cigarette paper pasted to the back of the cigarette paper you show your audience.

Take two papers, put a small amount of white paste onto one end of one of them and stick the other on top.

When the paste is dry, screw one of the pieces into a small ball. You may find the paste shows through, but don't worry; simply keep a finger over it.

Tear the whole paper into pieces and screw them up tightly as you open up the intact ball.

The small wad of torn pieces will remain at the back of the restored strip.

Show both hands empty, fingers apart. Then put the paper into one of your pockets. This will prevent any of your audience picking it up later and learning how your trick is done.

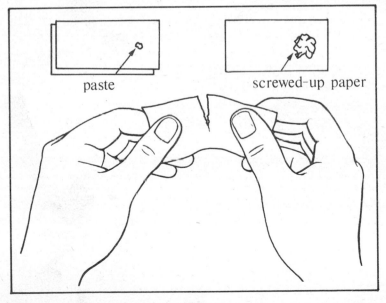

paste   screwed-up paper

The Torn Cigarette Paper (full version)

What you do

This fuller routine is an extension of the previous trick and a clever one.

Carry out the moves just as they have been described in the last trick and then announce that you have been given special permission by the Magic Circle to show everyone how the trick is done.

'As you probably have guessed, you need two pieces of paper,' you announce. 'I take a cigarette paper and have it hidden in my fingers throughout the trick. I then tear up this second paper, roll up the pieces and hide them between my fingers. Then, all I have to do is to produce the whole cigarette paper which I've kept hidden all the time, and I have magically restored the torn pieces into one whole strip.'

While talking, you are carrying out the moves you describe. Then comes the pay-off. Take the little wad of torn cigarette paper, still between your fingers, and remark, 'While here, of course, I have all the torn bits of paper.'

But, unbelievably, there are no torn pieces, the paper is whole again.

How you do it

This full version is well worth the extra effort needed to master the moves.

The explanation is, of course, that the piece of cigarette paper you show the audience and hide in your fingers is a normal piece of paper, quite unprepared.

Just hold it between your fingers so that it protrudes a little and the audience can see it for themselves throughout your performance.

The second cigarette paper (the one you tear up) *has* been prepared as outlined on the previous page. Thus, it is a simple matter for you to restore the torn pieces as a final pay-off at the end of the trick.

Your audience will be completely fooled if you carry out these moves smoothly. Take your time and make sure your words fit your movements.

'hidden' cigarette papers

Remove a Waistcoat without Removing the Jacket

What you do

This is a good fun trick at any party and is not at all difficult to perform.

Invite a male assistant to join you from the audience and announce that you will take off his waistcoat without removing his jacket.

Follow the instructions on the opposite page and practise the moves a few times. You will find no difficulty in carrying out your intention.

Make sure your assistant is wearing a waistcoat before you start and that his jacket sleeves are wide enough for you to get your hand up his arm. Take a good look at the width of his jacket cuffs before you start. If you can't find a victim with wide cuffs, then don't attempt the trick.

How you do it

First unbutton the waistcoat and then, if there is a strap at the back, check that it is unbuckled. Place your hands underneath his jacket and take hold of the edge of the waistcoat at the back.

Tell your assistant to extend both his arms at full length over his head. Then raise the bottom of his waistcoat over his head; you may have to force this if the garment is tight. He can now return his arms to his sides.

The waistcoat will now be across his chest. Take the right bottom end and put it into the arm-hole of the jacket at the shoulder. At the same time put your hand up his sleeve, and get hold of the waistcoat and pull it down the sleeve. This will release the arm-hole of the waistcoat.

Then pull the waistcoat back again out of the sleeve of the coat and put the same end of the waistcoat into the left arm-hole of the jacket.

Put your hand up the sleeve of the jacket in the same way as you did before and now you will be able to draw the whole waistcoat down the sleeve and out of the jacket.

The Concorde Coin

What you do

Place a 10p piece in each hand, palm upwards.

Announce that you will now cause something mysterious to happen. Put both hands flat on a cloth-covered table and lift up your right hand to show that it is empty.

However, on lifting up the left hand your audience will be astonished to see that this hand now contains two 10p pieces. The one that you had in your left hand has mysteriously flown through space with the speed of Concorde.

You can do the same effect sitting down and causing the coin in the right hand to vanish from the top of one leg on to the other.

The principle is the same in each case.

How you do it

The explanation is that you first have a coin on the edge of each palm just below the little fingers.

The coin in the left hand is thrown straight down on the table. The coin in the right hand is literally thrown across

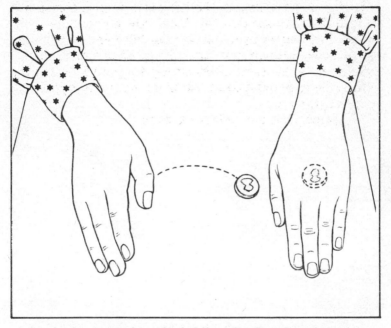

and quickly covered by the left hand's downward motion.

Try this out a few times and you will find it very easy to do. But have the audience in front of you; the coin's swift flight can sometimes be seen sideways.

Once you have the two coins safely under your left hand, lift up the right hand, keep it closed and pretend to throw an invisible coin across to the other hand, still flat on the table.

'Didn't you see it travel?' you can ask. 'No wonder. It's faster than Concorde.'

The Cunning Corks

What you do

Take two corks, one in each hand, and hold them between forefinger and thumb as shown in the picture (A).

Ask a friend if he thinks it possible for one cork to pass through the other.

Unless he knows the secret he is bound to admit that it looks an impossibility.

However, with apparent ease, you are able to retain each cork between thumb and forefinger and still separate your two hands.

Now challenge him to do the same!

How you do it

The corks have to be passed through each other in a special way which is quite mystifying. First, hold the corks as shown in the first picture.

Then turn the back of your left hand and the palm of your right hand towards you. Place the thumb of your left hand on the end of the right cork and the thumb of your right hand on the left cork.

Next, put the middle left-hand finger (B) on the end of the cork in the right hand and the right forefinger on the end of the cork in the left hand.

You can see what happens in the second picture.

Now move your hands apart and you will have both corks free of each other.

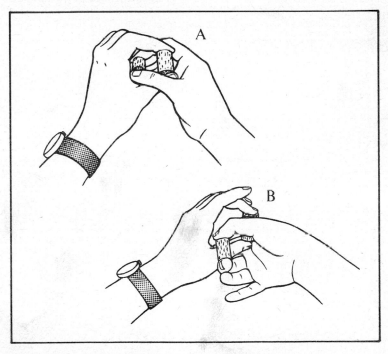

Torn and Restored Card

What you do

This is another fine trick which needs a certain amount of skill — and practice. After a few months of magic though, any teenage magician should be able to master it easily.

You get someone to select a card. Then tear the card in pieces and hand one corner back to the person to retain.

Put the rest of the pieces in an ashtray and set them alight. Leave the ashes in the tray and take an orange or grapefruit from your table.

Cut open the fruit and there, in the centre, is the chosen card — with one corner missing.

To prove it is the same card, take the torn piece from your assistant and show that it fits perfectly.

This is a classic trick and should not be attempted until you have become an experienced performer. Even if you never perform this trick yourself, carefully guard the secret of how it is done.

How you do it

First, you must learn to force a card, i.e., to make a spectator take the card you want him or her to take. This requires a certain advanced sleight of hand technique which you will find described in many books on card tricks obtainable from your bookseller or your public library.

For a beginner in magic, the easiest way is to buy a trick pack from a magical dealer. This will enable you to force a card without sleight of hand.

Use this special pack to force your card. Then you must put the trick pack in your right-hand jacket pocket and bring out a normal pack with backs matching the other pack. Show the faces of this second pack casually as you place it back on your table. This will establish in the minds of your audience that they had a genuine choice when they selected the card.

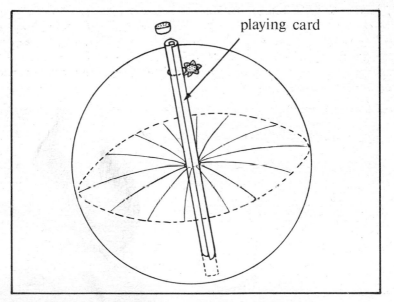

playing card

Let's assume you intend making your assistant take the ten of hearts. Before your performance you take a duplicate ten of hearts and tear off one corner. Roll up the rest of the card (you'll find this easy to do if you hold the card first in the steam of a kettle). Now take an orange or grapefruit and remove the little round part on the top of the fruit to the left of the stalk. Push a pencil through at this spot and insert your rolled-up playing card. Now carefully fasten the small blob of skin back into position using a small drop of glue or rubber cement.

When you cut open the fruit remember to cut it in half crosswise, *not* top to bottom, and your audience will see the card sticking upwards when you open up the two halves.

Have the torn piece of the duplicate card already hidden in your hand when your assistant hands you his torn pieces and just make sure you hand him back *your* piece for him to hold.

Otherwise, when the ten of hearts is magically restored with its corner missing, you will find his piece doesn't fit at all.